**All patterns** in this book may be worked with Peyote Stitch or Brick Stitch. I personally bead the rectangular designs with Peyote Stitch.

The only ones I recommend Brick Stitch for is the Mermaid tail and the Night Wings patterns on pages 8-11 and 22-25.

## Basic Brick Stitch Instructions

Row 1

Row one base row: Usually the middle or widest row is the base row unless indicated otherwise on the pattern. Pick up 2 beads on your needle and position them toward the end of the thread. Holding beads in place with your thumb and forefinger, run the needle thru them again in same direction making a circle.

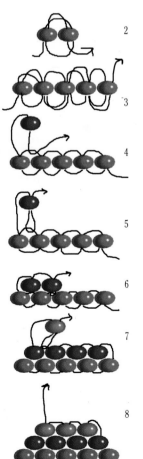

# Design Index

Gazing
Pages 4 - 5

Back of Gazing
Pages 6 - 7

Ships at Sea
Pages 8 - 11

Beached
Pages 12 - 13

Fishy
Pages 14 - 15

Silhouette
Pages 16 -17

Waiting
Pages 18 - 19

3 Backs
Pages 20 - 21

Night Wings
Pages 22 - 25

Tapestry
Pages 26 - 27

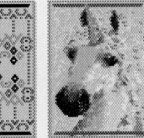
Back of Mystic
Pages 28 - 29

Mystic Morn
Pages 30 - 31

Back of Fairy
Pages 32 - 33

Fairy Blue
Pages 34 - 35

Pull the circle tight positioning the 2 beads side by side.

Continue adding more beads until you have the total you need for the base row.

Turn work around. Always work from left to right. For the second row, with a bead on the thread, bring the needle through the top loop that goes between the last 2 beads of the very first row.

Pull the bead into place. Bring the needle back up through the bead coming up through the bottom and pull it down.

If the thread is pulled too tight, the beadwork becomes rigid and warped. Just pull up the slack until the bead is snug. Continue to add beads as shown to the end of the row.

Turn and continue in the same manner for the remaining rows.

Weave the thread through the finished work, clip the thread close to the beads.

## Joining Seams

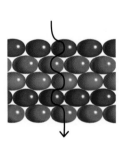

To join a peyote stitch with a 'zipper' join, have both of your edges meet with the beads alternating on either side so they will interlock like a zipper. Take your thread through the first end bead, through the next bead that fits into the 'zipper' on the other side and continue this way, pulling on the thread every 3 or 4 stitches. Don't pull too tight or your work will warp.

## Ideas for Fringe

When you string the fringe, all the bead holes are facing down, so the strands of fringe will hang straight down from the bag, forming two side by side rows of thick fringe.

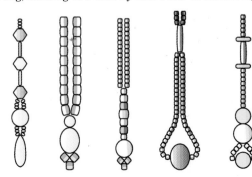

# Gazing

*This pretty pattern makes up into a very lovely purse or it can be framed for a wallhanging. In the sample, handmade lampwork glass beads pick up the apricot and rose tones in her gown.*

Stitch: Peyote or Brick          Size: Approximately 3½" x 4½"          Beads Used: Delica

**Begin Here** - work Peyote Stitch beginning with this row. Work from left to right across the pattern.

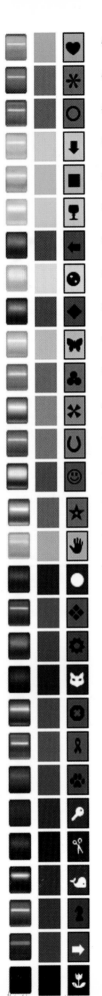

#54 - Lined Rainbow Topaz Rose - 114 beads

#69 - Lined Rainbow Crystal Tan - 72 beads

#102 - Metallic Luster Rose Gold 28 beads

#205 - Opaque Pearl Beige - 65 beads

#208 - Opaque Tan - 137 beads

#233 - Lined Luster Crystal Apricot - 46 beads

#380 - Matte Metallic Luster Green Pink - 51 beads

#883 - Matte Rainbow Opaque Ivory 100 beads

#884 - Matte Opaque Rainbow Brown - 41 beads

#211 - Opaque Alabaster - 24 beads

#100 - Transparent Rainbow Light Topaz - 70 beads

#411 - Galvanized Bright Gold 114 beads

#256 - Lined Opaque Crystal Taupe 85 beads

#31 - Opaque Metallic 24 kt Bright Gold - 106 beads

#35 - Galvanized Silver - 21 beads

#52 - Lined Rainbow Crystal Ivory - 72 beads

#301 - Matte Opaque Blue Grey 299 beads

#61 - Lined Rainbow Topaz - 193 beads

#865 - Matte Rainbow Transparent Smoke Topaz - 90 beads

#323 - Matte Metallic Iris Purple - 79 beads

#022L - Opaque Metallic Light Bronze - 23 beads

#122 - Light Brown Iris 101 beads

#794 - Dyed Matte Opaque Red - 45 beads

#773 - Dyed Matte Transparent Cherry - 104 beads

#325 - Transparent Rainbow Light Topaz - 571 beads

#23 - Galvanized Bright Gold 243 beads

#108 - Lined Opaque Crystal Taupe 68 beads

#105 - Metallic Luster Ruby Gold - 568 beads

#310 - Matte Opaque Black 942 beads

For straps and embellishments, gather your own collection of beads, natural stones and crystals. Plan a design that makes the bag uniquely yours. Note: The bead quantities given do not include fringe and strap.

Bag by Deb Bergs
Peach lampwork in strap and fringe by Juanita Floyd Shadow Wolf Studio
Leesburg, VA 20176
rvnsbrk@aol.com

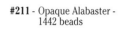

#211 - Opaque Alabaster - 1442 beads

#105 - Metallic Luster Ruby Gold - 1494 beads

#310 - Opaque Matte Black - 1212 beads

#410 - Galvanized Bright Gold - 324 beads

*You'll love beading this intricate Celtic looking design and it is really easy to stitch. This creation makes a bold yet feminine fashion statement.*

For straps and embellishments, gather your own collection of beads, natural stones and crystals. Plan a design that makes the bag uniquely yours. Note: The bead quantities given do not include fringe and strap.

Bag by Deb Bergs
Peach lampwork in strap and fringe by
Juanita Floyd
Shadow Wolf Studio
Leesburg, VA 20176
rvnsbrk@aol.com

# Back of Gazing

*Very dramatic in the colors shown, this is an easy design to stitch. These colors match the Gazing pattern. Substitute your own colors for a totally different look!*

Stitch: Peyote or Brick          Size: Approximately 3½" x 4½"          Beads Used: Delica

**Begin Here** - work Peyote Stitch beginning with this row. Work from left to right across the pattern.

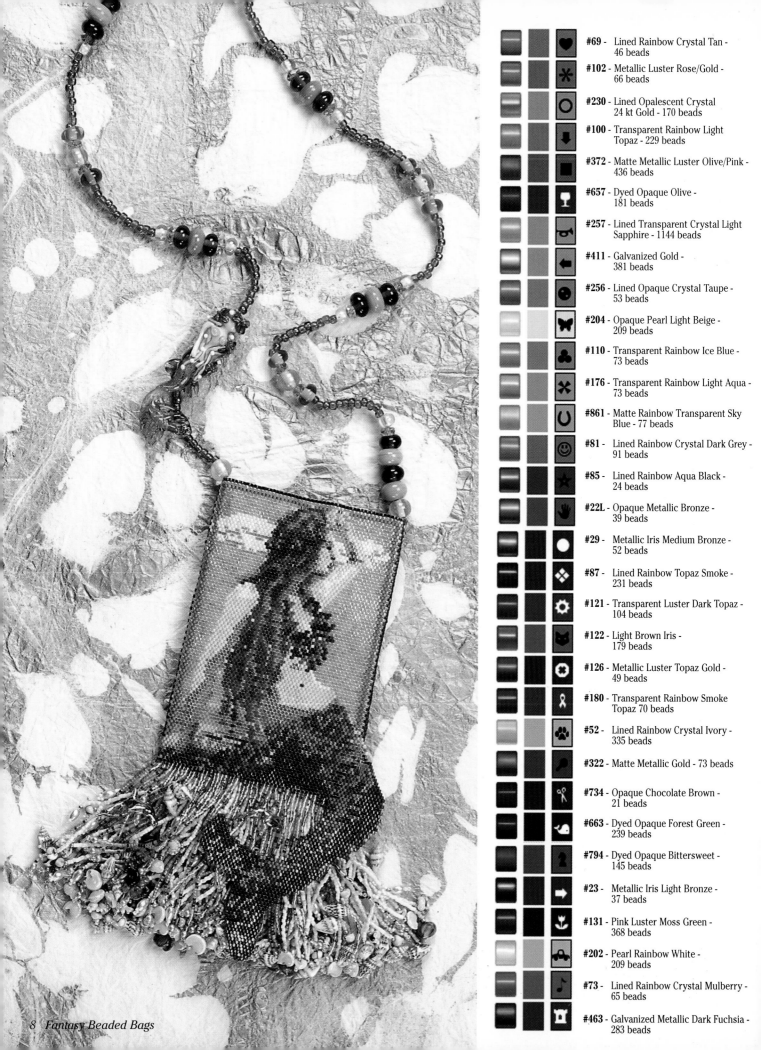

| | | | |
|---|---|---|---|
| | | ♥ | **#69** - Lined Rainbow Crystal Tan - 46 beads |
| | | ✳ | **#102** - Metallic Luster Rose/Gold - 66 beads |
| | | ○ | **#230** - Lined Opalescent Crystal 24 kt Gold - 170 beads |
| | | ↓ | **#100** - Transparent Rainbow Light Topaz - 229 beads |
| | | ■ | **#372** - Matte Metallic Luster Olive/Pink - 436 beads |
| | | ♆ | **#657** - Dyed Opaque Olive - 181 beads |
| | | ⚷ | **#257** - Lined Transparent Crystal Light Sapphire - 1144 beads |
| | | ← | **#411** - Galvanized Gold - 381 beads |
| | | ◉ | **#256** - Lined Opaque Crystal Taupe - 53 beads |
| | | 🦋 | **#204** - Opaque Pearl Light Beige - 209 beads |
| | | ♣ | **#110** - Transparent Rainbow Ice Blue - 73 beads |
| | | ❋ | **#176** - Transparent Rainbow Light Aqua - 73 beads |
| | | ℧ | **#861** - Matte Rainbow Transparent Sky Blue - 77 beads |
| | | ☺ | **#81** - Lined Rainbow Crystal Dark Grey - 91 beads |
| | | ★ | **#85** - Lined Rainbow Aqua Black - 24 beads |
| | | ✋ | **#22L** - Opaque Metallic Bronze - 39 beads |
| | | ● | **#29** - Metallic Iris Medium Bronze - 52 beads |
| | | ◈ | **#87** - Lined Rainbow Topaz Smoke - 231 beads |
| | | ✿ | **#121** - Transparent Luster Dark Topaz - 104 beads |
| | | 🐱 | **#122** - Light Brown Iris - 179 beads |
| | | ✪ | **#126** - Metallic Luster Topaz Gold - 49 beads |
| | | ⚕ | **#180** - Transparent Rainbow Smoke Topaz 70 beads |
| | | 🐾 | **#52** - Lined Rainbow Crystal Ivory - 335 beads |
| | | 🔑 | **#322** - Matte Metallic Gold - 73 beads |
| | | ✂ | **#734** - Opaque Chocolate Brown - 21 beads |
| | | 🐋 | **#663** - Dyed Opaque Forest Green - 239 beads |
| | | ? | **#794** - Dyed Opaque Bittersweet - 145 beads |
| | | → | **#23** - Metallic Iris Light Bronze - 37 beads |
| | | 🌷 | **#131** - Pink Luster Moss Green - 368 beads |
| | | 🚗 | **#202** - Pearl Rainbow White - 209 beads |
| | | ♪ | **#73** - Lined Rainbow Crystal Mulberry - 65 beads |
| | | ⊡ | **#463** - Galvanized Metallic Dark Fuchsia - 283 beads |

# Ships at Sea

*This unique design adds a free-form element… the mermaid's tail. Stitch the body of the bag using normal peyote and then add the tail element using brick stitch. The tail will appear to be part of the design of the back as well.*

Stitch: Brick          Size: Approximately 4" x 7½"          Beads Used: Delica

**Begin Here** - work Peyote Stitch beginning with this row. Work from left to right across the pattern.

The Tail chart is continued on page 11.

*Front of Ships at Sea*

*Beached Back of Ships at Sea*

| | | | | |
|---|---|---|---|---|
| | | ♥ | **#69** - | Lined Rainbow Crystal Tan - 46 beads |
| | | ✳ | **#102** - | Metallic Luster Rose/Gold - 66 beads |
| | | ○ | **#230** - | Lined Opalescent Crystal 24 kt Gold - 170 beads |
| | | ↓ | **#100** - | Transparent Rainbow Light Topaz - 229 beads |
| | | ■ | **#372** - | Matte Metallic Luster Olive/Pink - 436 beads |
| | | ♉ | **#657** - | Dyed Opaque Olive - 181 beads |
| | | 📯 | **#257** - | Lined Transparent Crystal Light Sapphire - 1144 beads |
| | | ← | **#411** - | Galvanized Gold - 81 beads |
| | | ☻ | **#256** - | Lined Opaque Crystal Taupe - 53 beads |
| | | 🦋 | **#204** - | Opaque Pearl Light Beige - 209 beads |
| | | ♣ | **#110** - | Transparent Rainbow Ice Blue - 73 beads |
| | | ❋ | **#176** - | Transparent Rainbow Light Aqua - 73 beads |
| | | ↻ | **#861** - | Matte Rainbow Transparent Sky Blue - 77 beads |
| | | ☺ | **#81** - | Lined Rainbow Crystal Dark Grey - 91 beads |
| | | ★ | **#85** - | Lined Rainbow Aqua Black - 24 beads |
| | | ✋ | **#22L** - | Opaque Metallic Bronze - 39 beads |
| | | ● | **#29** - | Metallic Iris Medium Bronze - 52 beads |
| | | ❖ | **#87** - | Lined Rainbow Topaz Smoke - 231 beads |
| | | ✿ | **#121** - | Transparent Luster Dark Topaz - 104 beads |
| | | 🐱 | **#122** - | Light Brown Iris - 179 beads |
| | | ✾ | **#126** - | Metallic Luster Topaz Gold - 49 beads |
| | | ⚲ | **#180** - | Transparent Rainbow Smoke Topaz - 70 beads |
| | | 🐾 | **#52** - | Lined Rainbow Crystal Ivory - 335 beads |
| | | 🔑 | **#322** - | Matte Metallic Gold - 73 beads |
| | | ✂ | **#734** - | Opaque Chocolate Brown - 21 beads |
| | | 🐦 | **#663** - | Dyed Opaque Forest Green - 239 beads |
| | | 🔑 | **#794** - | Dyed Opaque Bittersweet - 145 beads |
| | | → | **#23** - | Metallic Iris Light Bronze - 37 beads |
| | | 🌷 | **#131** - | Pink Luster Moss Green - 368 beads |
| | | 🔒 | **#202** - | Pearl Rainbow White - 09 beads |
| | | ♪ | **#73** - | Lined Rainbow Crystal Mulberry - 65 beads |
| | | 🏺 | **#463** - | Galvanized Metallic Dark Fuchsia - 283 beads |

# Ships at Sea

**C**ontinued from page 9

Here's the chart for the free-form element… the mermaid's tail. Stitch the body of the bag using normal Peyote. Add the tail element using Brick Stitch. The tail will appear to be part of the design of the back as well.

For straps and embellishments, gather your own collection of beads, natural stones and crystals. Plan a design that makes the bag uniquely yours. Note: The bead quantities given do not include fringe and strap.

The Tail Chart

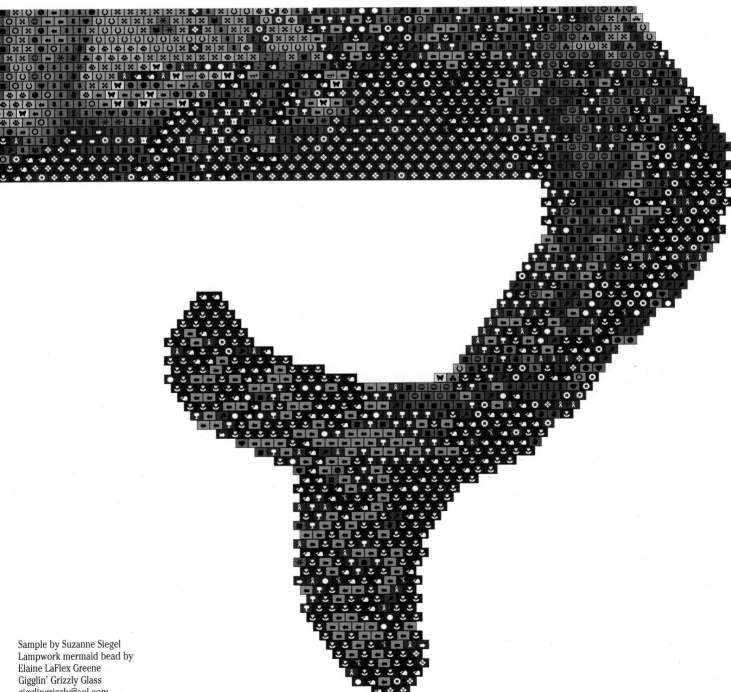

Sample by Suzanne Siegel
Lampwork mermaid bead by
Elaine LaFlex Greene
Gigglin' Grizzly Glass
gigglingrizzly@aol.com

# Beached
## Back of Ships at Sea

*The tail element on the front of this bag becomes part of the back design creating a truly unique piece of artwork!.*

Stitch: Peyote or Brick          Size: Approximately 4" x 7½"          Beads Used: Delica

**Begin Here** - work Peyote Stitch beginning with this row. Work from left to right across the pattern.

#69 - Lined Rainbow Crystal Tan - 46 beads

#102 - Metallic luster Rose Gold - 84 beads

#230 - Lined Opalescent Crystal 24 kt. Gold - 199 beads

#100 - Transparent Rainbow Light Topaz - 32 beads

#372 - Matte Luster Olive /Pink - 363 beads

#657 - Dyed Opaque Olive - 82 beads

#257 - Lined Transparent Crystal Light - Sapphire - 260beads

#411 - Galvanized Gold - 237 beads

#256 - Lined Opaque Crystal Taupe - 125 beads

#204 - Opaque Pearl Light Beige - 191 beads

#110 - Transparent Rainbow Ice Blue- 70 beads

#81 - Lined Rainbow Crystal Dark Grey - 43 beads

#85- Lined Rainbow Aqua Black - 82 beads

#22L - Opaque Metallic Light Bronze - 117 beads

#29 - Metallic Iris Medium Bronze - 35 beads

#87 - Lined Rainbow Smoke Topaz - 122 beads

#121 - Transparent Luster Dark Topaz - 47 beads

#122 - Light Brown Iris - 15 beads

#126 - Metallic Luster Top[az Gold - 49 beads

#180 - Transparent Rainbow Smoke Topaz - 56 beads

#52 - Lined Rainbow Crystal Ivory - 249 beads

#322 - Matte Metallic Gold - 94 beads

#734 - Opaque Chocolate Brown - 96 beads

#794 - Dyed Matte Red - 71 beads

#23 - Metallic Iris Light Brown - 11 beads

#202 - Pearl Rainbow White- 153 beads

#463 - Galvanized Metallic Dark Fuschia - 269 beads

#203 - Opaque Pearl Light Yellow - 226 beads

For straps and embellishments, gather your own collection of beads, natural stones and crystals. Plan a design that makes the bag uniquely yours. Note: The bead quantities given do not include fringe and strap.

#205 - Opaque Pearl Beige - 129 beads

#352 - Matte Opaque Cream - 404 beads

#354 - Matte Opaque Flesh Pink - 238 beads

#234 - Lined Luster Crystal Light Pink - 106 beads

#351 - Matte Opaque White - 80beads

#86 - Lined Rainbow Crystal Jet - 102beads

#310 - Matte Opaque Black - 145 beads

#131 - Lined Luster Crystal Light Pink - 52 beads

Sample by Suzanne Siegel
PO Box 2152
Kalispell, MT 59903
ssiegel@cyberport.net

# Something Fishy

*This is a simple pattern to finish and you can embellish it in so many ways! I used a pretty lampwork mermaid, but you could use small shells, fish beads and other 'fishy' items!*

Stitch: Peyote or Brick          Size: Approximately 2½" x 3"          Beads Used: Delica

**Begin Here** - work Peyote Stitch beginning with this row. Work from left to right across the pattern.

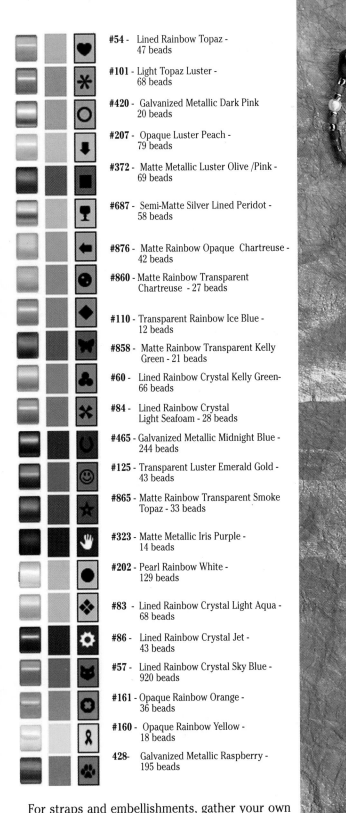

#54 - Lined Rainbow Topaz - 47 beads

#101 - Light Topaz Luster - 68 beads

#420 - Galvanized Metallic Dark Pink 20 beads

#207 - Opaque Luster Peach - 79 beads

#372 - Matte Metallic Luster Olive /Pink - 69 beads

#687 - Semi-Matte Silver Lined Peridot - 58 beads

#876 - Matte Rainbow Opaque Chartreuse - 42 beads

#860 - Matte Rainbow Transparent Chartreuse - 27 beads

#110 - Transparent Rainbow Ice Blue - 12 beads

#858 - Matte Rainbow Transparent Kelly Green - 21 beads

#60 - Lined Rainbow Crystal Kelly Green- 66 beads

#84 - Lined Rainbow Crystal Light Seafoam - 28 beads

#465 - Galvanized Metallic Midnight Blue - 244 beads

#125 - Transparent Luster Emerald Gold - 43 beads

#865 - Matte Rainbow Transparent Smoke Topaz - 33 beads

#323 - Matte Metallic Iris Purple - 14 beads

#202 - Pearl Rainbow White - 129 beads

#83 - Lined Rainbow Crystal Light Aqua - 68 beads

#86 - Lined Rainbow Crystal Jet - 43 beads

#57 - Lined Rainbow Crystal Sky Blue - 920 beads

#161 - Opaque Rainbow Orange - 36 beads

#160 - Opaque Rainbow Yellow - 18 beads

428- Galvanized Metallic Raspberry - 195 beads

For straps and embellishments, gather your own collection of beads, natural stones and crystals. Plan a design that makes the bag uniquely yours. Note: The bead quantities given do not include fringe and strap.

Bag by Deb Bergs
Lampwork mermaid bead by Elaine LaFlex Greene
Gigglin' Grizzly Glass
gigglingrizzly@aol.com
Enamel starfish by The String Bead
Wausau, WI
705-849-5696

# Silhouette

*A unicorn shown only in shadows and highlights, how lovely! Use with Celtic Knot #3 or a solid back, decorate with charms and pearls and finish with a bright handmade dichroic bead with a unicorn in its depths!*

Stitch: Peyote or Brick          Size: Approximately 2½" x 3"          Beads Used: Delica

**Begin Here** - work Peyote Stitch beginning with this row. Work from left to right across the pattern.

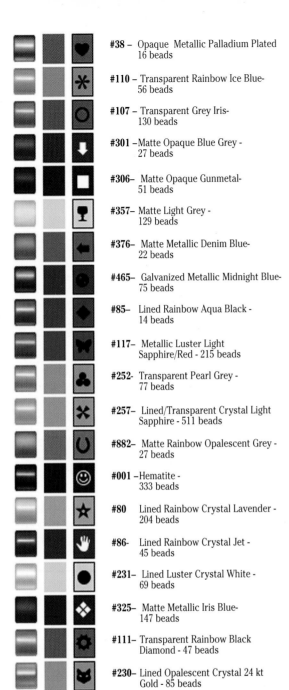

| | | | |
|---|---|---|---|
| | | ♥ | **#38** – Opaque Metallic Palladium Plated 16 beads |
| | | ✳ | **#110** – Transparent Rainbow Ice Blue- 56 beads |
| | | ○ | **#107** – Transparent Grey Iris- 130 beads |
| | | ⬇ | **#301** –Matte Opaque Blue Grey - 27 beads |
| | | ◻ | **#306**– Matte Opaque Gunmetal- 51 beads |
| | | 🍷 | **#357**– Matte Light Grey - 129 beads |
| | | ⬅ | **#376**– Matte Metallic Denim Blue- 22 beads |
| | | ◉ | **#465**– Galvanized Metallic Midnight Blue- 75 beads |
| | | ◆ | **#85**– Lined Rainbow Aqua Black - 14 beads |
| | | 🦋 | **#117**– Metallic Luster Light Sapphire/Red - 215 beads |
| | | ♣ | **#252**– Transparent Pearl Grey - 77 beads |
| | | ✳ | **#257**– Lined/Transparent Crystal Light Sapphire - 511 beads |
| | | ☡ | **#882**– Matte Rainbow Opalescent Grey - 27 beads |
| | | ☺ | **#001** –Hematite - 333 beads |
| | | ☆ | **#80** Lined Rainbow Crystal Lavender - 204 beads |
| | | ✋ | **#86**- Lined Rainbow Crystal Jet - 45 beads |
| | | ● | **#231**– Lined Luster Crystal White - 69 beads |
| | | ◈ | **#325**– Matte Metallic Iris Blue- 147 beads |
| | | ✿ | **#111**– Transparent Rainbow Black Diamond - 47 beads |
| | | 🐱 | **#230**– Lined Opalescent Crystal 24 kt Gold - 85 beads |

For straps and embellishments, gather your own collection of beads, natural stones and crystals. Plan a design that makes the bag uniquely yours. Note: The bead quantities given do not include fringe and strap.

Bag by Deb Bergs
Unicorn dichroic lampwork by Linda Greene
Copper Moon Cat
703-383-9083, coppery164@cs.com

# Waiting

*A little fairy maiden sits on a pebble, perhaps waiting for the first flowers of spring or maybe for a friend to come and join her in a dance! The design is the same size as those in my first book and the backs from that book will work with this design as well.*

Bag by Roberta Dildine
B & D Designs
bddildine@designsbydeb.com

Fairy bead by Elaine LaFlex Greene
Gigglin' Grizzly Glass
gigglingrizzly@aol.com

Stitch: Peyote or Brick          Size: Approximately 2½" x 3          Beads Used: Delica

**Begin Here** - work Peyote Stitch beginning with this row. Work from left to right across the pattern.

For straps and embellishments, gather your own collection of beads, natural stones and crystals. Plan a design that makes the bag uniquely yours. Note: The bead quantities given do not include fringe and strap.

#69 - Lined Rainbow Crystal Tan - 30 beads

#102 - Metallic Luster Rose Gold - 54 beads

#417 - Galvanized Metallic Pale Lilac - 26 beads

#857 - Matte Rainbow Transparent Light Amethyst - 27 beads

#863 - Matte Rainbow Transparent Grey - 30 beads

#884 - Matte Opaque Rainbow Brown - 42 beads

#230 - Lined Opal Crystal 24 kt Gold - 72 beads

#100 - Transparent Rainbow Light Topaz - 50 beads

#256 - Lined Opalescent Crystal Taupe - 57 beads

#411 - Galvanized Gold - 54 beads

#31 - Opaque Metallic 24 kt Bright Gold - 57 beads

#52 - Lined Rainbow Crystal Ivory - 52 beads

#176 - Transparent Rainbow Light Aqua - 610 beads

#234 - Lined Crystal Light Pink - 63 beads

#465 - Galvanized Metallic Midnight Blue - 368 beads

#730 - Opaque Medium Blue - 21 beads

#881 - Matte Rainbow Opalescent Periwinkle - 42 beads

#61 - Lined Rainbow Topaz Amethyst - 191 beads

#158 - Opaque Rainbow Lilac - 29 beads

#210 - Opaque Luster Old Rose - 43 beads

#244 - Opalescent Pearl Light Pink - 48 beads

#379 - Matte Metallic Lavender - 39 beads

#758 - Matte Opaque Lilac - 24 beads

#765 - Matte Transparent Lilac - 16 beads

#865 - Matte Rainbow Transparent Smoke Topaz - 40 beads

#22L - Opaque Metallic Light Bronze - 31 beads

#322 - Matte Metallic Gold - 27 beads

#864 - Matte Rainbow Transparent Cobalt - 24 beads

#80 - Lined Rainbow Crystal Lavender - 60 beads

#325 - Matte Metallic Iris Blue - 31 beads

#178 - Transparent Rainbow Sapphire - 22 beads

# Back of Silhouette

*While this design appears very complex, it is actually very easy! Use the colors shown or substitute another color scheme for a unique look all your own... just replace them with your own shadings!*

Bag by Deb Bergs
Unicorn dichroic
lampwork by
Linda Greene
Copper Moon Cat
703-383-9083
coppery164@cs.com

**Begin Here** - work Peyote Stitch beginning with this row. Work from left to right across the pattern.

# Back of Waiting

*This back design can be made in a variety of colors, simply select a range and then substitute colors going from light to dark. The colors shown match the Waiting pattern.*

Bag by Deb Bergs
Lampwork mermaid bead
by Elaine LaFlex Greene
Gigglin' Grizzly Glass
gigglingrizzly@aol.com
Enamel starfish by
The String Bead
Wausau, WI
705-849-5696

**Begin Here** - work Peyote Stitch beginning with this row. Work from left to right across the pattern.

#117 - Metallic Luster Light Sapphire Red - 1120 beads

#231 - Lined Luster Crystal White - 219 beads

#80 - Lined Rainbow Crystal Lavender - 695 beads

#252 - Transparent Pearl Grey - 246 beads

## For the Backs of All Bags

**Stitch:**
Peyote or Brick

**Size:**
Approximately
2½" x 3

**Beads Used:** Delica

For straps and embellishments, gather your own collection of beads, natural stones and crystals. Plan a design that makes the bag uniquely yours. Note: The bead quantities given do not include fringe and strap.

#176 - Transparent Rainbow Light Aqua - 376 beads

#234 - Lined Luster Crystal Light Pink - 202 beads

#465 - Galvanized Metallic Midnight Blue - 999 beads

#61 - Lined Rainbow Topaz Amethyst – 167 beads

#210 - Opaque Luster Old Rose - 205 beads

#244 - Opaque Pearl Light Pink - 331 beads

# Back of Something Fishy

*This back design looks complicated but is very simple and uses just 3 colors! The colors giving match the Something Fishy pattern.*

Bag by Deb Bergs
Lampwork mermaid bead by
Elaine LaFlex Greene
Gigglin' Grizzly Glass
gigglingrizzly@aol.com
Enamel starfish by
The String Bead
Wausau, WI
705-849-5696

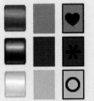

#428 - Galvanized Metallic Raspberry - 192 beads

#465 - Galvanized Metallic Midnight Blue - 1164 beads

#202 - Pearl Rainbow White - 924 beads

**Begin Here** - work Peyote Stitch beginning with this row. Work from left to right across the pattern.

# Night Wings

This design can be finished either as a bib type necklace or as a wallhanging to be framed or hung from a rod or other object. Because of its size, it will be heavy when finished, so be sure to use several strands of thread for the necklace to avoid breakage.

For straps and embellishments, gather your own collection of beads, natural stones and crystals. Plan a design that makes the bag uniquely yours. Note: The bead quantities given do not include fringe and strap.

Bag by Deb Atkins
The Bead Hive
Wichita, KS 76213
316-264-6616
D7442039@aol.com

*Pattern on page 24 & 25*

# Tapestry Unicorn

*Use this larger design as a wall hanging or for a jacket or purse. While it looks complex, it actually uses few colors and is quite simple to make!*

For straps and embellishments, gather your own collection of beads, natural stones and crystals. Plan a design that makes the bag uniquely yours. Note: The bead quantities given do not include fringe and strap.

Bag by Dawn Marvin
Mourning Dove Makings
Wichita, KS
mourningdovemakes@hotmail.com

*Pattern on page 26 & 27*

# Night Wings

*This design can be finished either as a bib type necklace or as a wallhanging to be framed or hung from a rod or other object. Because of its size it will be heavy when finished, so be sure to use several strands of thread for the necklace to avoid breakage.*

Stitch: Peyote or Brick

Size: Approximately 6½" x 8½"

Beads Used: Delica

by Deb Atkins
The Bead Hive
Wichita, KS 76213
316-264-6616
D7442039@aol.com

| | | |
|---|---|---|
| ❤ | #203 - | Opaque Pearl Light Yellow - 80 beads |
| ✳ | #205 - | Opaque Pearl Beige - 25 beads |
| ◯ | #380 - | Matte Metallic Luster Green Pink - 41 beads |
| ↓ | #857 - | Matte Rainbow Transparent Light Amethyst - 31 beads |
| ■ | #863 - | Matte Rainbow Transparent Grey - 59 beads |
| ♟ | #884 - | Matte Opaque Rainbow Brown - 155 beads |
| ← | #234 - | Lined/Luster Light Pink - 45 beads |
| ◉ | #462 - | Galvanized Metallic Dark Grey Mauve - 16 beads |
| ◆ | #410 - | Galvanized Bright Gold - 185 beads |
| 🦋 | #123 - | Transparent Luster Olive Grey - 62 beads |
| ♣ | #256 - | Lined Opalescent Crystal Taupe - 22 beads |
| ✾ | #351 - | Matte White - 180 beads |
| ∪ | #35 - | Galvanized Silver - 1109 beads |
| ☺ | #52 - | Lined Rainbow Crystal Ivory - 23 beads |
| ★ | #110 - | Transparent Rainbow Ice Blue - 639 beads |
| ✋ | #107 - | Transparent Grey Iris - 272 beads |
| ● | #301 - | Matte Opaque Blue Grey - 120 beads |
| ◈ | #307 - | Matte Opaque Grey - 175 beads |
| ✿ | #376 - | Matte Metallic Denim Blue - 35 beads |
| ☆ | #310 - | Matte Black - 4003 beads |
| ♠ | #871 - | Matte Opalescent Rainbow Jet - 346 beads |
| ✪ | #451 - | Galvanized Metallic Denim Blue - 1068 beads |
| 🎗 | #117 - | Metallic Luster Light Sapphire/Red 1071 beads |
| 🐾 | #158 - | Opaque Rainbow Lilac - 124 beads |
| 🔑 | #241 - | Transparent Pearl Pale Lavender - 614 beads |
| ✂ | #252 - | Transparent Pearl Grey - 207 beads |
| 🐌 | #257 - | Lined/Transparent Crystal Light Sapphire - 11 beads |
| 🔓 | #356 - | Matte Opalescent Lavender - 89 beads |

**Begin Here** - work Peyote Stitch beginning with this row. Work from left to right across the pattern.

J...

| | | |
|---|---|---|
| ➡ | #379 - | Matte Metallic Lavender - 100 beads |
| 🌷 | #419 - | Galvanized Metallic Lilac - 24 beads |
| 🚗 | #454 - | Galvanized Metallic Light Grape - 109 beads |
| ♪ | #882 - | Matte Rainbow Opalescent Grey - 271 beads |
| 🏰 | #323 - | Matte Metallic Iris Purple - 239 beads |
| 🎺 | #29 - | Metallic Iris Medium Bronze - 115 beads |
| ≈ | #201 - | Opaque Pearl White - 241 beads |
| ★ | #111 - | Transparent Rainbow Black Diamond - 187 beads |
| L | #104 - | Transparent Iris Raspberry - 42 beads |

For straps and embellishments, gather your own collection of beads, natural stones and crystals. Plan a design that makes the bag uniquely yours. Note: The bead quantities given do not include fringe and strap.

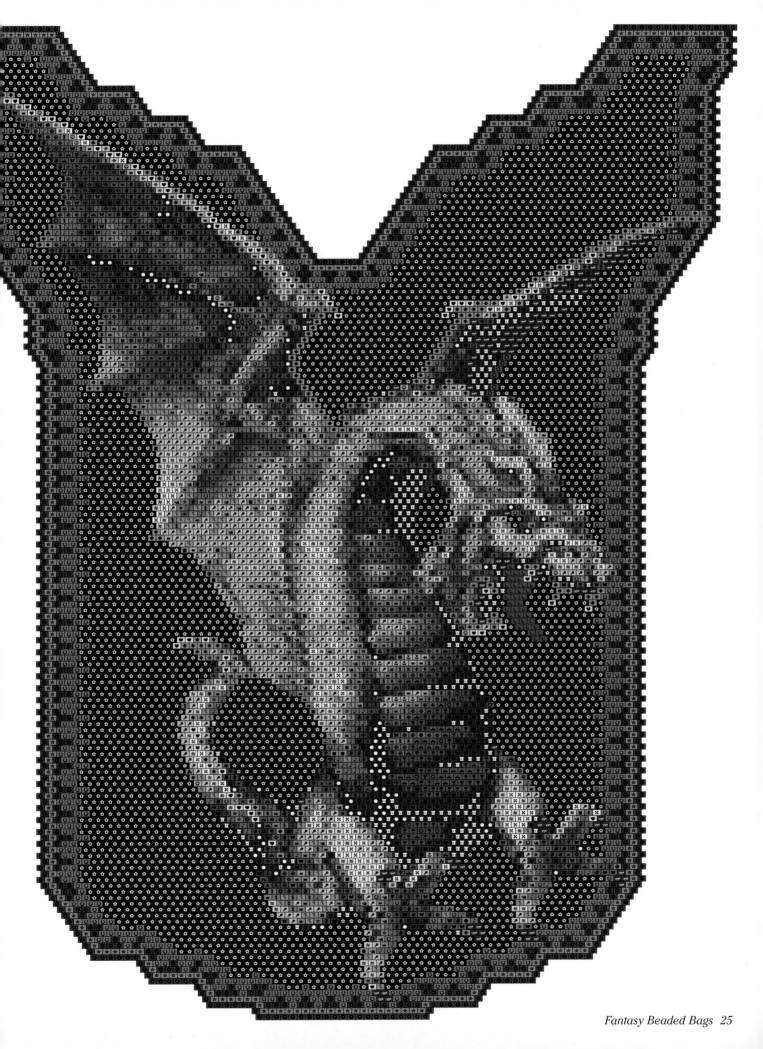

• •**Begin Here** - work Peyote Stitch beginning with this row.
• • Work from left to right across the pattern.

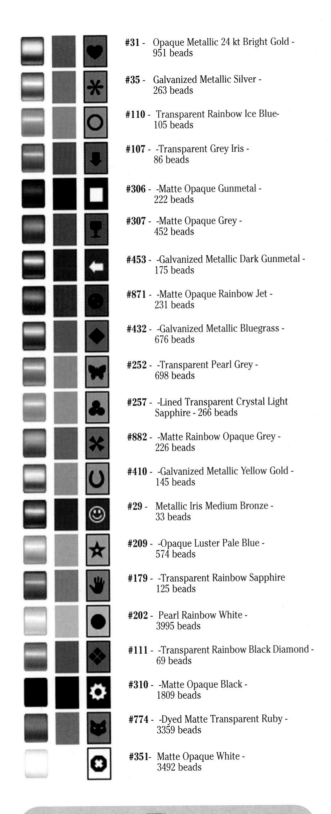

#31 - Opaque Metallic 24 kt Bright Gold - 951 beads

#35 - Galvanized Metallic Silver - 263 beads

#110 - Transparent Rainbow Ice Blue - 105 beads

#107 - -Transparent Grey Iris - 86 beads

#306 - -Matte Opaque Gunmetal - 222 beads

#307 - -Matte Opaque Grey - 452 beads

#453 - -Galvanized Metallic Dark Gunmetal - 175 beads

#871 - -Matte Opaque Rainbow Jet - 231 beads

#432 - -Galvanized Metallic Bluegrass - 676 beads

#252 - -Transparent Pearl Grey - 698 beads

#257 - -Lined Transparent Crystal Light Sapphire - 266 beads

#882 - -Matte Rainbow Opaque Grey - 226 beads

#410 - -Galvanized Metallic Yellow Gold - 145 beads

#29 - Metallic Iris Medium Bronze - 33 beads

#209 - -Opaque Luster Pale Blue - 574 beads

#179 - -Transparent Rainbow Sapphire 125 beads

#202 - Pearl Rainbow White - 3995 beads

#111 - -Transparent Rainbow Black Diamond - 69 beads

#310 - -Matte Opaque Black - 1809 beads

#774 - -Dyed Matte Transparent Ruby - 3359 beads

#351- Matte Opaque White - 3492 beads

## Tip:
For ease in pattern translation, ask your copy shop to enlarge patterns to 200%.

# Tapestry Unicorn

*Use this larger design as a wallhanging or for a jacket or purse. While it looks complex, it actually uses few colors and is quite simple to make!*

Stitch: Peyote or Brick

Size: Approximately 7" x 9"

Beads Used: Delica

For straps and embellishments, gather your own collection of beads, natural stones and crystals. Plan a design that makes the bag uniquely yours. Note: The bead quantities given do not include fringe and strap.

by Dawn Marvin
Mourning Dove Makings
Wichita, KS
mourningdovemakes@hotmail.com

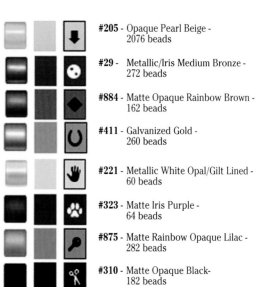

**#205** - Opaque Pearl Beige - 2076 beads

**#29** - Metallic/Iris Medium Bronze - 272 beads

**#884** - Matte Opaque Rainbow Brown - 162 beads

**#411** - Galvanized Gold - 260 beads

**#221** - Metallic White Opal/Gilt Lined - 60 beads

**#323** - Matte Iris Purple - 64 beads

**#875** - Matte Rainbow Opaque Lilac - 282 beads

**#310** - Matte Opaque Black - 182 beads

For straps and embellishments, gather your own collection of beads, natural stones and crystals. Plan a design that makes the bag uniquely yours. Note: The bead quantities given do not include fringe and strap.

Bag by Deb Bergs
Unicorn lampwork and floral accent beads by
LandS Art
808-623-3102
landsart.com

# Back of Mystic Morn

*An arrangement of stylized flowers reminiscent of a Persian rug is the perfect back design for elegant Mystic Morn!*

Stitch: Peyote or Brick          Size: Approximately 3¾" x 4¼"          Beads Used: Delica

**Begin Here** - work Peyote Stitch beginning with this row. Work from left to right across the pattern.

29

# Mystic Morn

*Done in soft shades of tan, peach, rose and white, Mystic Morn is very elegant. Deep wine-colored pearls and hand made lampwork beads add the perfect finishing touches!*

**Stitch:** Peyote or Brick          **Size:** Approximately 3¾" x 4¼"          **Beads Used:** Delica

**Begin Here** - work Peyote Stitch beginning with this row.
Work from left to right across the pattern.

For straps and embellishments, gather your own collection of beads, natural stones and crystals.
Plan a design that makes the bag uniquely yours. Note: The bead quantities given do not include fringe and strap.

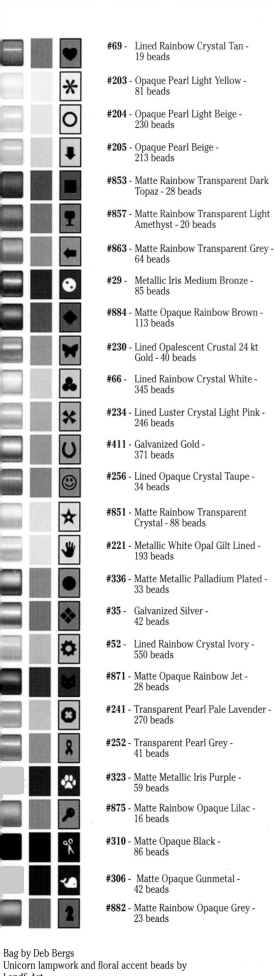

**#69** - Lined Rainbow Crystal Tan - 19 beads

**#203** - Opaque Pearl Light Yellow - 81 beads

**#204** - Opaque Pearl Light Beige - 230 beads

**#205** - Opaque Pearl Beige - 213 beads

**#853** - Matte Rainbow Transparent Dark Topaz - 28 beads

**#857** - Matte Rainbow Transparent Light Amethyst - 20 beads

**#863** - Matte Rainbow Transparent Grey - 64 beads

**#29** - Metallic Iris Medium Bronze - 85 beads

**#884** - Matte Opaque Rainbow Brown - 113 beads

**#230** - Lined Opalescent Crustal 24 kt Gold - 40 beads

**#66** - Lined Rainbow Crystal White - 345 beads

**#234** - Lined Luster Crystal Light Pink - 246 beads

**#411** - Galvanized Gold - 371 beads

**#256** - Lined Opaque Crystal Taupe - 34 beads

**#851** - Matte Rainbow Transparent Crystal - 88 beads

**#221** - Metallic White Opal Gilt Lined - 193 beads

**#336** - Matte Metallic Palladium Plated - 33 beads

**#35** - Galvanized Silver - 42 beads

**#52** - Lined Rainbow Crystal Ivory - 550 beads

**#871** - Matte Opaque Rainbow Jet - 28 beads

**#241** - Transparent Pearl Pale Lavender - 270 beads

**#252** - Transparent Pearl Grey - 41 beads

**#323** - Matte Metallic Iris Purple - 59 beads

**#875** - Matte Rainbow Opaque Lilac - 16 beads

**#310** - Matte Opaque Black - 86 beads

**#306** - Matte Opaque Gunmetal - 42 beads

**#882** - Matte Rainbow Opaque Grey - 23 beads

Bag by Deb Bergs
Unicorn lampwork and floral accent beads by
LandS Art
808-623-3102
landsart.com

| | | ♥ | **#117** - Metallic Luster Topaz Red - 845 beads |
| | | * | **#257** - Lined Transparent Crystal Ligh[t] Sapphire - 54 beads |
| | | ○ | **#29** - Metallic Iris Medium Bronze - 478 beads |
| | | ↓ | **#200** - Chalk White - 1685 beads |
| | | □ | **#377** - Matte Metallic Denim Blue - 287 beads |
| | | ♎ | **#411** - Galvanized Gold - 375 beads |

For straps and embellishments, gather your own collection of beads, natural stones and crystals. Plan a design that makes the bag uniquely yours. Note: The bead quantities given do not include fringe and strap.

Bag by Kathy Atkinson
Wichita, KS
kea1275@yahoo.com

# Back of Fairy in Blue

*An abstract floral design in blues and purples graces the back of the Fairy in Blue.*

Stitch: Peyote or Brick          Size: Approximately 3½" x 4"          Beads Used: Delica

Work from left to right across the pattern.

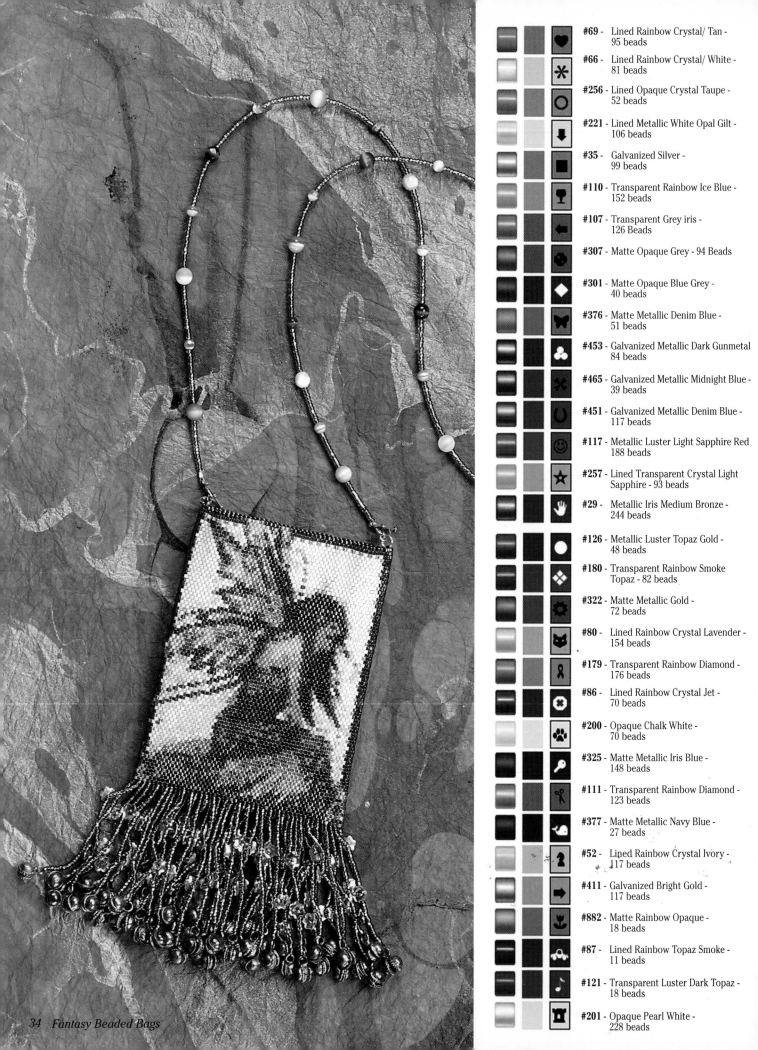

| | | | | |
|---|---|---|---|---|
| | | ♥ | **#69** - | Lined Rainbow Crystal/ Tan - 95 beads |
| | | ✳ | **#66** - | Lined Rainbow Crystal/ White - 81 beads |
| | | ⬭ | **#256** - | Lined Opaque Crystal Taupe - 52 beads |
| | | ⬇ | **#221** - | Lined Metallic White Opal Gilt - 106 beads |
| | | ■ | **#35** - | Galvanized Silver - 99 beads |
| | | 🍷 | **#110** - | Transparent Rainbow Ice Blue - 152 beads |
| | | ← | **#107** - | Transparent Grey iris - 126 Beads |
| | | 🐟 | **#307** - | Matte Opaque Grey - 94 Beads |
| | | ◆ | **#301** - | Matte Opaque Blue Grey - 40 beads |
| | | 🦋 | **#376** - | Matte Metallic Denim Blue - 51 beads |
| | | ♣ | **#453** - | Galvanized Metallic Dark Gunmetal 84 beads |
| | | ✳ | **#465** - | Galvanized Metallic Midnight Blue - 39 beads |
| | | ⊔ | **#451** - | Galvanized Metallic Denim Blue - 117 beads |
| | | ☺ | **#117** - | Metallic Luster Light Sapphire Red 188 beads |
| | | ★ | **#257** - | Lined Transparent Crystal Light Sapphire - 93 beads |
| | | ✋ | **#29** - | Metallic Iris Medium Bronze - 244 beads |
| | | ● | **#126** - | Metallic Luster Topaz Gold - 48 beads |
| | | ❖ | **#180** - | Transparent Rainbow Smoke Topaz - 82 beads |
| | | ⚙ | **#322** - | Matte Metallic Gold - 72 beads |
| | | 🐱 | **#80** - | Lined Rainbow Crystal Lavender - 154 beads |
| | | 🎗 | **#179** - | Transparent Rainbow Diamond - 176 beads |
| | | ✲ | **#86** - | Lined Rainbow Crystal Jet - 70 beads |
| | | 🐾 | **#200** - | Opaque Chalk White - 70 beads |
| | | 🔑 | **#325** - | Matte Metallic Iris Blue - 148 beads |
| | | ✂ | **#111** - | Transparent Rainbow Diamond - 123 beads |
| | | 🐋 | **#377** - | Matte Metallic Navy Blue - 27 beads |
| | | 🔑 | **#52** - | Lined Rainbow Crystal Ivory - 117 beads |
| | | → | **#411** - | Galvanized Bright Gold - 117 beads |
| | | 🌷 | **#882** - | Matte Rainbow Opaque - 18 beads |
| | | 🚗 | **#87** - | Lined Rainbow Topaz Smoke - 11 beads |
| | | ♪ | **#121** - | Transparent Luster Dark Topaz - 18 beads |
| | | ♟ | **#201** - | Opaque Pearl White - 228 beads |